D1367852

THE BEST
EXTREME
SPORTS STARS
OF ALL TIME

By Matt Scheff

www.abdopublishing.com

Published by Abdo Publishing, a division of ABDO, PO Box 398166, Minneapolis, Minnesota 55439. Copyright © 2015 by Abdo Consulting Group, Inc. International copyrights reserved in all countries. No part of this book may be reproduced in any form without written permission from the publisher. SportsZone™ is a trademark and logo of Abdo Publishing.

Printed in the United States of America, North Mankato, Minnesota
092014
012015

Cover Photos: Arno Balzarini/AP Images, right; Ricardo Arduengo/AP Images, left
Interior Photos: Arno Balzarini/AP Images, 1 (right); Ricardo Arduengo/AP Images, 1 (left); Chris Polk/AP Images, 7, 35, 41; Tony Donaldson/Icon SMI/Newscom, 9, 19, 21, 27, 31, 33; Sports File/Icon SMI/Newscom, 11, 13; Diane Moore/Icon SMI/Newscom, 15, 17; Jarvis Gray/Shutterstock Images, 23; Christopher Halloran/Shutterstock Images, 25; Dan Loh/AP Images, 29; Mark J. Terrill/AP Images, 37, 49, 55; Tass/ABACA/Newscom, 39; Christophe Ena/AP Images, 43; Shutterstock Images, 45; Lionel Cironneau/AP Images, 47; Warren Price Photography/Shutterstock Images, 51; Brian Ciancio/ZUMA Press/Newscom, 53; Josh Chapel/ZUMApress/Newscom, 57; Bret Hartman/AP Images, 59; Cody York Photography, 61

Editor: Patrick Donnelly
Series Designer: Christa Schneider

Library of Congress Control Number: 2014944203

Cataloging-in-Publication Data
Scheff, Matt.
 The best extreme sports stars of all time / Matt Scheff.
   p. cm. -- (Sports' best ever)
ISBN 978-1-62403-618-7 (lib. bdg.)
Includes bibliographical references and index.
1. Extreme sports--Juvenile literature.   I. Title.
796.04--dc23

                              2014944203

TABLE OF CONTENTS

INTRODUCTION

Extreme athletes push their sports to the limit.

Snowboarders flip, spin, and twist their way down giant ramps. Motocross riders soar through the air. And surfers, bicycle motocross (BMX) riders, skateboarders, and others amaze fans with their fantastic tricks.

Who are the legends of action sports? They are the men and women who have taken their sports to a new level. They have landed tricks that no one thought possible. They have pulled off the most difficult technical feats and made them look easy. And they have turned small, little-known sports into mainstream sensations.

Here are some of the best extreme sports stars of all time.

TONY HAWK

Tony Hawk had something special planned for the best trick competition at the 1999 X Games. The skateboarding sensation did not want to just do something amazing. He wanted to make history.

Hawk dropped into the vert ramp and built up his speed. Then he launched himself into the air. He spun 900 degrees—two and a half spins—in midair. No vert skater had ever landed a 900 in competition. Hawk wanted to be the first.

But he crashed. Again and again, Hawk tried to land the 900. Ten straight times, he failed. He was out of time. Hawk's chance to land a 900 in competition was over. But he still went for it one more time. He whizzed down the ramp on his board in a blur of motion, launched himself, and started spinning . . .

Tony Hawk slides along a rail during vert practice at the 2003 X Games.

Then he landed safely back on the ramp. The crowd went wild! The legend of Tony Hawk had just grown a little bigger.

In action sports, there are superstars, and then there is Hawk. More than any other athlete, Hawk took action sports into the mainstream. He made difficult tricks look effortless with his smooth style. And he made new tricks possible with his innovative and daring approach.

Hawk started riding a skateboard at age nine. He turned pro at age 14. By the late 1980s, he was the biggest thing in skateboarding. He won gold in the vert competition at the first X Games in 1995.

Hawk was at the peak of his career in 1999. But after he landed his amazing 900, he shocked his fans by retiring. Hawk remained a big part of the skating scene. But his days as a full-time pro were over. He walked away leaving no doubt as to who is the greatest skateboarder of all time.

103

The number of pro skateboarding contests Tony Hawk entered by age 25. He won 73 of them and placed second in 19 more.

Tony Hawk competes at the 1999 X Games in San Francisco.

TONY HAWK

Sport: Skateboarding

Hometown: San Diego, California

Height: 6 feet 3 inches

Weight: 171 pounds

Birth Date: May 12, 1968

X Games: 10 gold medals
Vert (1995, 1997)
Vert Doubles (1997–2002)
Vert Best Trick (1999, 2003)

BARRETT CHRISTY

Barrett Christy worked her way down the slopestyle course at the 1997 Winter X Games. The powder swished under her snowboard. She built up some speed, launched over a jump, and thrilled the audience with a front flip. Christy was in control—sailing, spinning, and getting huge air to impress the judges. It was a gold-medal run. She went on to win another gold in the big air competition. That helped cement her place as the best all-around female snowboarder in the world.

Christy did not even discover snowboarding until she was an adult. But once she stepped onto a board, there was no turning back. Fans loved her clean, creative style. She could string together trick combinations few other snowboarders would even attempt. And fans especially loved her signature trick, the Barrett Roll. It is a front flip with a 180-degree spin.

Barrett Christy in action at the 1998 US Open Snowboard Championships in Stratton, Vermont.

Christy's career lasted only a decade. But what she achieved in that time was amazing. Christy was twice named *Transworld Riders*'s Best Overall Female Snowboarder. She even competed in the 2003 women's snowboard superpipe event while she was pregnant with her first child.

Christy left competitive snowboarding after she began a family. But she remains active in the community. She helps design boards for Gnu Snowboards. Christy was one of the first female action sports stars. Her career helped pave the way for future generations of women on the slopes.

11

Barrett Christy's X Games medal count. She won more medals than any other snowboarder in X Games history through 2014.

Barrett Christy got a late start, but she soon became one of the biggest stars in snowboarding.

BARRETT CHRISTY

Sport: Snowboarding

Hometown: Bucks County, Pennsylvania

Height: 5 feet 2

Weight: 110 pounds

Birth Date: February 3, 1971

X Games: 4 gold medals
Big Air (1997, 1999 Summer, 1999 Winter)
Slopestyle (1997)

JEREMY McGRATH

Jeremy McGrath's dirt bike slammed down onto the track. He revved his motor. Dirt flew up from his rear tire. It was 1993, his first full season in the American Motocross Association (AMA) Supercross 250. McGrath had his sights on the leader. The young rider roared down a straightaway and drove his bike hard into a turn. The crowd roared as McGrath passed defending champ Jeff Stanton. McGrath crossed the finish line with his first supercross victory. Many more would follow.

McGrath turned pro when he was just 15 years old. With masterful control of his bike, he was an instant success. He started out by winning several regional supercross championships in 1991 and 1992. And from the moment he started racing in the AMA 250 circuit in 1993, the sport was never the same.

Jeremy McGrath in action during a 1999 race in San Bernardino, California

Few athletes have ever dominated their sport the way McGrath dominated supercross in the 1990s. From 1993 to 2000, he won seven of the eight AMA 250 titles. At times, he seemed to be in a league of his own. Nicknamed the "King of Supercross," McGrath's star power took the sport to new heights. Even today, his reign is called the "McGrath Era."

McGrath was at his best on the tight, compact tracks of supercross. But he was also a force on the longer, more open courses of motocross. McGrath won the 1995 AMA Motocross 250 title, proving he was a true all-purpose rider. After he retired from dirt bike racing in 2006, he turned to off-road truck racing. But no matter what else he might accomplish, one thing is certain. McGrath will always stand as one of the greatest dirt bike racers in history.

72

Jeremy McGrath's win total in AMA Supercross—the most in the sport's history through 2014.

Jeremy McGrath gets big air at a 2003 AMA Supercross event in Anaheim, California.

JEREMY McGRATH

Sport: Motocross

Hometown: San Diego, California

Height: 5 feet 8

Weight: 160 pounds

Birth Date: November 19, 1971

Championships: 8
AMA Supercross: 7 (1993–96, 1998–2000)
AMA Motocross: 1 (1995)

X Games: 1 gold medal
Moto X Step Up (2004)

MAT HOFFMAN

Mat Hoffman was a BMX great long before he dropped into the vert ramp at the 2002 X Games. But what he did that day made him a true legend. Hoffman built up speed with a few big airs. Then he prepared to try a trick he had dreamed of doing for 13 years. Hoffman sailed high over the ramp as he spun around two and a half times. And he did it no-handed! The crowd erupted as Hoffman landed the amazing trick.

Hoffman joined the freestyle BMX circuit in 1987 at age 15. At the time, freestyle BMX was a small, little-known sport. But Hoffman set out to change that. His daring, inventive moves gave the sport its first real star. In 1989, he became the first rider ever to land a 900 in competition. His high-flying style earned him the nickname "The Condor."

Mat Hoffman performs a trick at the 2010 Old School BMX Freestyle Reunion.

Hoffman was a true trendsetter.

He invented trick after trick, and not just in BMX freestyle. He also blazed new trails in streetstyle. And in the 1990s, he invented the idea of BMX big air. It involves performing a single trick per run on an oversized ramp. His amazing 24-foot (7.3 m) air off a 20-foot (6.1 m) ramp helped launch a whole new style of riding. The X Games introduced the big air event in 2005.

Hoffman also became a pop-culture star. He had his own video game line called *Mat Hoffman's Pro BMX*. He was a regular on MTV. And he helped produce several films. Hoffman even made headlines in 1999 when he jumped his bike off of a 3,500-foot (1.1 km) cliff with a parachute. Hoffman never competed in another X Games after his famous no-handed 900. But he remains a force in the sport and is a living BMX legend.

50

The world-record height in feet (15.3 m) that Mat Hoffman jumped his bike in 2002.

Mat Hoffman thrills the crowd at the 2000 X Games in San Francisco.

MAT HOFFMAN

Sport: BMX Freestyle

Hometown: Oklahoma City, Oklahoma

Height: 6 feet

Weight: 160 pounds

Birth Date: January 9, 1972

X Games: 2 gold medals
  BMX freestyle vert (1995, 1996)

KELLY SLATER

The sun was shining and the surf was perfect. Kelly Slater was making his final run of the 2005 Billabong Tahiti Pro. He had already wowed the crowd by scoring a rare perfect 10 on his first wave. Another good wave could seal the title.

Slater spotted a wave coming in and got ready. He stood on his board as the wave began to crest. It was a beautiful 6-foot (1.8 m) barrel. Slater carved out a smooth, flawless ride, dancing his board through the wave. He scored another 10 for a perfect total of 20. No one else had done that before.

"King Kelly" is surfing royalty. He has been entering—and winning—surfing competitions since he was eight years old. In 1992, Slater became the youngest world champion at age 21.

Kelly Slater has been on top of the surfing world since 1992.

Slater's powerful build, flexibility, and incredible board control amazed fans and fellow surfers. He seemed able to turn harder and sharper than anyone else, and his ability to recover from a stumble was unmatched. Slater's raw skill and his constant willingness to go big helped redefine what could be done with a surfboard.

Surfing has always been dominated by young riders. But age has not slowed Slater down. He still routinely beats competitors half his age. In 2011, he won his eleventh Association of Surfing Professionals (ASP) world title. No one else has close to that many. And in 2013, he thrilled surfing fans everywhere when he scored the second perfect 20 of his career at age 41. Slater's influence on the sport is as strong as ever. He has inspired a generation of surfers. When he is not catching a wave, he is busy designing some of the most popular surfboards in the world.

5

The number of consecutive world titles Kelly Slater won from 1994 through 1998.

Kelly Slater competes in the Nike US Open of Surfing in Huntington Beach, California, in 2012.

KELLY SLATER

Sport: Surfing

Hometown: Cocoa Beach, Florida

Height: 5 feet 9

Weight: 160 pounds

Birth Date: February 11, 1972

Championships: 11 ASP World Tour titles (1992, 1994–98, 2005, 2006, 2008, 2010, 2011)

DAVE MIRRA

All eyes were on rising BMX freestyle star Dave Mirra. He stood at the top of the ramp next to teammate Dennis McCoy. Mirra had already won the 1998 X Games BMX vert and BMX park events in thrilling fashion. Now he prepared to drop in with McCoy for their second run in the vert doubles event.

Their first run had been a disaster. They needed something big on their second and final run to win gold. Mirra had just the trick. He built up some speed. Then he skied his bike toward McCoy. The crowd gasped as Mirra tapped his rear tire on McCoy's back. It was a one-of-a-kind trick. The judges rewarded the pair with another gold. And Mirra became the first athlete ever to win gold in three different events at a single X Games.

Dave Mirra in action at the 1998 X Games in San Diego

From the time he was four years old, Mirra was on a bike. He turned pro while still a teenager. And he quickly became the sport's biggest star. Mirra made headlines at the 2000 X Games when he landed the first double backflip in BMX freestyle history. He was the face of his sport for more than a decade before injuries forced him to give it up.

In 2010, Mirra switched his focus to a form of auto racing called rally racing. His best X Games finish in RallyCross was fourth, in 2011. But fans of the "Miracle Man" know better than to doubt that he might one day add to his impressive medal count.

24

Dave Mirra's X Games medal count—a record that stood until 2013.

Dave Mirra was a driving force in the sport of BMX freestyle for more than a decade.

DAVE MIRRA

Sport: BMX Freestyle

Hometown: Chittenango, New York

Height: 5 feet 9

Weight: 155 pounds

Birth Date: April 4, 1974

X Games: 11 individual gold medals
Freestyle Vert (1997, 1999, 2001, 2001, 2004)
Freestyle Park (1996, 1997, 1999, 2000, 2004, 2005)

BLAIR
MORGAN

Snocross legend Blair Morgan worked his way through a busy pack. It was the final of the 2006 Winter X Games snocross event. Morgan raced his Ski-Doo snowmobile down a straightaway and into second place. Leader Levi LaVallee was out front with a big lead. On the last lap, LaVallee sailed over a jump. But his sled came crashing down in a bad landing. LaVallee bounced off the sled. And Morgan whizzed by to win the race. It was his fifth X Games gold.

Morgan started his career in motocross in 1993. He won several Canadian national titles before switching his focus to snocross in 1997. On the snow, Morgan was an instant success. He changed the sport forever when he decided to stand on his running boards, rather than sit. With his unusual posture and high-flying moves, Morgan dominated snocross.

Blair Morgan flies high on his way to a snocross gold medal at the 2003 Winter X Games.

Fans nicknamed Morgan "Superman," not because he reminded them of the Man of Steel. He loved to do a trick called "the Superman" while sailing over a big jump.

Morgan was at his best at the Winter X Games. He won five gold medals from 2001 through 2006. But injuries began to slow him down. In 2008, Morgan was practicing for a supercross race at Olympic Stadium in Montreal, Canada. He lost control of his bike as he sailed over a jump. He crashed hard. The accident crushed two of the vertebrae in Morgan's back and left him paralyzed.

Morgan's career was over, but he remains a beloved figure in motor sports. Other supercross stars have honored Morgan by doing his famous Superman trick to celebrate big wins.

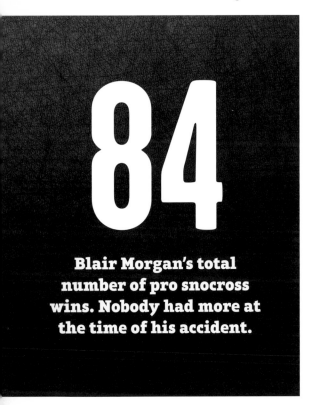

84

Blair Morgan's total number of pro snocross wins. Nobody had more at the time of his accident.

Blair Morgan shows off his gold medal at the 2003 Winter X Games.

BLAIR MORGAN

Hometown: Prince Albert, Saskatchewan, Canada

Height: 5 feet 11

Weight: 165 pounds

Birth Date: October 9, 1975

X Games: 5 gold medals
  Snocross (2001–2003, 2005, 2006)

TRAVIS PASTRANA

The Staples Center in Los Angeles was buzzing. Travis Pastrana rumbled up on his dirt bike. He was getting ready for his turn in the 2006 X Games Moto X best trick event. And everyone knew what he had planned. His fellow racers lined up, nervous and excited.

Pastrana's motor whined as he zipped toward the big dirt ramp. He sped up the ramp and launched into the air, pulling back on his handlebars. The dirt bike spun backward in the air for a complete backflip. And it kept going. Pastrana held the tight spin for a second backflip, completing it just in time for a safe landing. It was a double backflip! The entire arena went wild. Everyone knew they had just witnessed one of the most amazing moments in the history of freestyle motocross (FMX).

Travis Pastrana holds his gold medal after winning the motocross freestyle finals at the 2003 X Games.

It seems Pastrana can do anything on wheels. He was a championship motocross racer before turning to FMX. He landed his first backflip on a dirt bike in 2003. Then he did the double just three years later. Pastrana's eight career gold medals in FMX made him a legend. But he was not content to stop there. Pastrana turned to rally car racing. He won the Rally America National Series title four straight years from 2006 to 2009. Pastrana also raced in NASCAR's second-level series, posting a best finish of ninth.

In 2011, Pastrana married skateboarding star Lyn-Z Adams Hawkins. They travel the country together putting on an action sports show called Nitro Circus.

269

The distance in feet (82 m) that Pastrana jumped his rally car to set a world record. He broke the old mark by almost 100 feet (30 m).

Travis Pastrana is known throughout the freestyle motocross world for his high-flying tricks.

TRAVIS PASTRANA

Sports: Freestyle Motocross, Rally Car Racing

Hometown: Davidsonville, Maryland

Height: 6 feet 2

Weight: 205 pounds

Birth Date: October 8, 1983

X Games: 9 gold medals
Freestyle (1999–2001, 2003, 2005, 2006, 2010)
Best Trick (2006)
Speed and Style (2010)

TUCKER HIBBERT

Tucker Hibbert leaned over his snowmobile as he gunned the throttle. The sled roared down a straightaway and over a jump. Hibbert had leader Ross Martin in his sights. With a burst of speed, Hibbert blew past Martin to grab the lead. Nobody could catch him. Hibbert's sled roared across the finish line. He was the gold-medal winner in the 2013 Winter X Games snocross event.

Hibbert is the fastest man on snow. No racer in the world gets more out of his sled. Hibbert seems to nail every jump and turn on a course. And once he has a lead, he is almost impossible to catch.

Tucker Hibbert competes at the 2012 FIM Snowcross World Championship in Russia.

Hibbert has been racing snowmobiles and motorcycles since he was two years old. He turned pro in 2001 at age 17, then won the National Snocross Pro Open Championship as a rookie. Hibbert won his first X Games medal in 2002. But he soon left the sport to focus full-time on supercross and motocross racing.

Hibbert was a good motorcycle racer. But by 2006, he realized his future was in snowmobile racing. He returned to the sport and dominated as few ever have. Hibbert won his first Winter X Games snocross gold medal in 2007. He went on to win the next seven gold medals in that event (it was not held in 2012).

No one in the history of snocross has won more races than Hibbert. And when he is not out on the snow, Hibbert still enjoys racing dirt bikes. He is a true all-weather action sports star.

7

The number of consecutive Winter X Games snocross gold medals Tucker Hibbert won from 2007 to 2014. That is the longest streak in X Games history.

Tucker Hibbert gets some air while racing at the 2001 Winter X Games at Mount Snow, Vermont.

TUCKER HIBBERT

Sport: Snocross

Hometown: Pelican Rapids, Minnesota

Height: 6 feet

Weight: 165 pounds

Birth Date: June 24, 1984

X Games: 8 gold medals
Snocross (2000, 2007–11, 2013, 2014)

LINDSEY JACOBELLIS

Six riders burst out of the gate at the women's snowboard cross final at the 2014 Winter X Games. They remained in a tight bunch over the first jump. But on the second jump, Lindsey Jacobellis started to pull away.

It was a nearly flawless run. Jacobellis sailed over the jumps and sliced through the turns as she barreled down the track. Yet Eva Samkova was right on her heels. The two riders battled it out to the final jump. Jacobellis nailed it and crossed the finish line just a tenth of a second ahead of Samkova to claim the gold.

Jacobellis has been carving up snowboard cross—also called boardercross—courses since she first started competing at age 11. She won X Games gold in snowboard cross and bronze in slopestyle in 2003. Since then, she has dominated the sport.

Lindsey Jacobellis waves to the crowd after receiving her silver medal at the 2006 Winter Olympics in Turin, Italy.

Yet Jacobellis may be most famous for winning a silver medal—or losing a gold medal. In the 2006 Winter Olympics, she was cruising down the mountain with a huge lead. The gold medal was all but wrapped up. But on the last jump, she tried to pull a little trick in celebration. It backfired. Jacobellis fell, then stumbled to a second-place finish. Her tough luck in the Olympics popped up again four years later. She once again fell in a race she was leading. Then at the 2014 Olympics, Jacobellis was leading in the semifinals but fell. She did not even make the finals.

Despite those stumbles, there is no doubt Jacobellis is the greatest women's boardercross rider in history. And she shows no signs of slowing down any time soon.

8

The number of Winter X Games gold medals Lindsey Jacobellis has won through 2014.

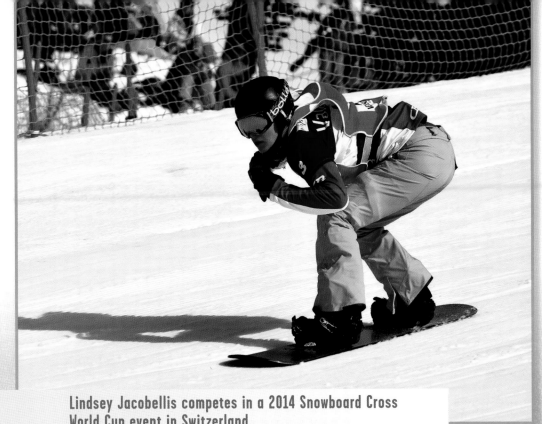

Lindsey Jacobellis competes in a 2014 Snowboard Cross World Cup event in Switzerland.

LINDSEY JACOBELLIS

Hometown: Stratton, Vermont

Height: 5 feet 6

Weight: 141 pounds

Birth Date: August 19, 1985

Olympics: Snowboard Cross 2006 (silver)

X Games: 8 gold medals
Snowboard Cross (2003–05, 2008–11, 2014)

SHAUN WHITE

Shaun White nailed his first run in the halfpipe finals at the 2010 Winter Olympics. The snowboarder had been in a league of his own since he turned pro 10 years earlier at age 13. Now he had already clinched his second Olympic gold medal. But one run still remained. White was ready to put on a show.

He started with a series of flawless flips, spins, and grabs. Then for his final trick, he blew out the biggest, most difficult move in the event. He sailed high over the ramp, flipped two times, then completed a dizzying three and a half spins before landing. It was a Double McTwist 1260! The crowd went wild. White sealed his status as the world's biggest snowboarding star.

Shaun White celebrates after winning gold in the halfpipe competition at the 2006 Winter Olympic Games.

"The Flying Tomato" got his nickname for his red hair and his amazing ability to get big air. Add his technical skill and fearless approach, and he is the ideal snowboarder.

White has dominated snowboarding for a decade and a half. He had 13 snowboarding gold medals in the Winter X Games through 2014. Those included six straight superpipe medals from 2008 to 2013. White also has starred at the Olympics. He earned gold in the halfpipe in 2006 and again in 2010. And he has blazed trails for new generations of snowboarders by pulling off tricks once thought impossible.

And if that were not enough, White is also a skateboarding star. White took home X Games gold in the vert in 2007 and again in 2011. That made him the first athlete to earn gold in different sports in the Summer and Winter X Games.

48.4

Shaun White's score on his second run at the 2010 Winter Olympics. It was the highest score in the history of the halfpipe.

Shaun White shows off his skateboarding skills while practicing for the 2006 X Games in Los Angeles.

SHAUN WHITE

Sports: Snowboarding and skateboarding

Hometown: San Diego, California

Height: 5 feet 9

Weight: 154 pounds

Birth Date: September 3, 1986

Olympics: Halfpipe 2006 (gold), 2010 (gold)

X Games: 15 gold medals
Superpipe (2003, 2006, 2008–13)
Slopestyle (2003–06, 2009)
Skateboard Vert (2007, 2011)

RYAN VILLOPOTO

Twenty-two engines roared as the 2014 Las Vegas Supercross began. Jake Weimer jumped out to the lead. But four-time champ Ryan Villopoto was close behind on his green Kawasaki. Villopoto dived hard into the first turn. Dirt spat up from behind his tires as he blew past Weimer for the lead. Villopoto powered down the straightaway. He sailed over a massive jump, then leaned into the next turn. Then he pulled away from the pack.

Villopoto may be the best dirt bike racer of all time. He has all the qualities the best racers need. He has amazing technical skills. He also knows how to run a flawless race. Nobody in the sport has better bike control. And he is fearless and aggressive on the track.

Ryan Villopoto races to victory at a 2008 race in Wortham, Texas.

Villopoto started off his pro career as the 2006 AMA Supercross/Motocross Rookie of the Year. He won his first championship a year later. That was the AMA National Motocross 250 title. He has been winning titles ever since.

250

The size of engine in cubic centimeters Ryan Villopoto used in the 2007 Motocross of Nations. He won two events against opponents using larger and faster 450cc engines.

Villopoto is a motocross star. But where he really shines is on the smaller, tighter courses of supercross. He won the AMA Supercross 450 championship four straight years from 2011 to 2014. No other rider had ever won more than two in a row. Villopoto has battled several serious injuries in his young career. But if he can stay healthy, he could rewrite all of the sport's record books before he is finished.

Ryan Villopoto hoists the champion's trophy after winning the 2014 AMA Supercross title.

RYAN VILLOPOTO

Sport: Motocross

Hometown: Poulsbo, Washington

Height: 5 feet 8

Weight: 155 pounds

Birth Date: August 13, 1988

Championships: 8
AMA Supercross: 4 (2011–14)
AMA Motocross: 4 (2007, 2008, 2011, 2013)

LYN-Z ADAMS
HAWKINS
PASTRANA

Lyn-Z Adams Hawkins dropped into the vert ramp for her run at the 2004 X Games. Hawkins was a rising star and looking for her first X Games gold medal. The run was nearly flawless. She nailed big trick after big trick. The biggest moment came when she launched herself high into the air. While sailing and spinning in the air, Hawkins kicked her board, caught it, then landed on it. The crowd roared. Hawkins had just done a Kick Flip Indy Grab. No woman had ever landed that trick in competition. Hawkins ran away with the gold.

Hawkins has been skateboarding since age two. She won her first X Games medal at age 14. And through 2014 she won two more golds in vert, in 2007 and 2009. One of her biggest accomplishments came in 2009. She became the first female skater to pull off a 540 McTwist.

Lyn-Z Adams Hawkins catches air during the vert final at the 2008 X Games.

Hawkins Pastrana—who married FMX star Travis Pastrana in 2011—has struggled with several severe injuries over her career. She has also taken some time away to start a family. But when she is healthy and skating, there is nobody better.

Few female skateboarders can match her combination of big air and fearlessness.

Hawkins Pastrana is also half of action sports' most famous couple. Lyn-Z and Travis travel around the world putting on a show called Nitro Circus, a popular festival centered on music and action sports. Fans know that when Hawkins Pastrana drops into the vert ramp, anything can happen.

55

The distance in feet (16.8 m) Lyn-Z Adams Hawkins Pastrana jumped when she became the first female skater ever to conquer the giant DC Mega Ramp.

Few women on the skateboarding circuit are as acrobatic and fearless as Lyn-Z Adams Hawkins Pastrana.

LYN-Z ADAMS HAWKINS PASTRANA

Sport: Skateboarding

Hometown: San Diego, California

Height: 5 feet 4

Weight: 120 pounds

Birth Date: September 21, 1989

X Games: 3 gold medals
Vert (2004, 2007, 2009)

NYJAH HUSTON

Nyjah Huston was in complete control at the 2014 X Games street final in Austin, Texas. He was already the leader when he began his second run. With his silky-smooth style, Huston landed one trick after another. In the final seconds of his run, he launched himself over some stairs. Huston spun in the air, came down on a handrail, and then sprung his board to the ground below. It was a flawless cab 270 backside lipslide. It was the perfect trick to end yet another gold-medal run for the world's best streetstyle skater.

Huston is a natural on a skateboard. He has been wowing audiences with his unique, free-flowing skating style since he was a kid. His board control is unmatched. Even when Huston goes big, he makes it look easy.

Nyjah Huston competes during the men's street final at the 2011 X Games in Los Angeles.

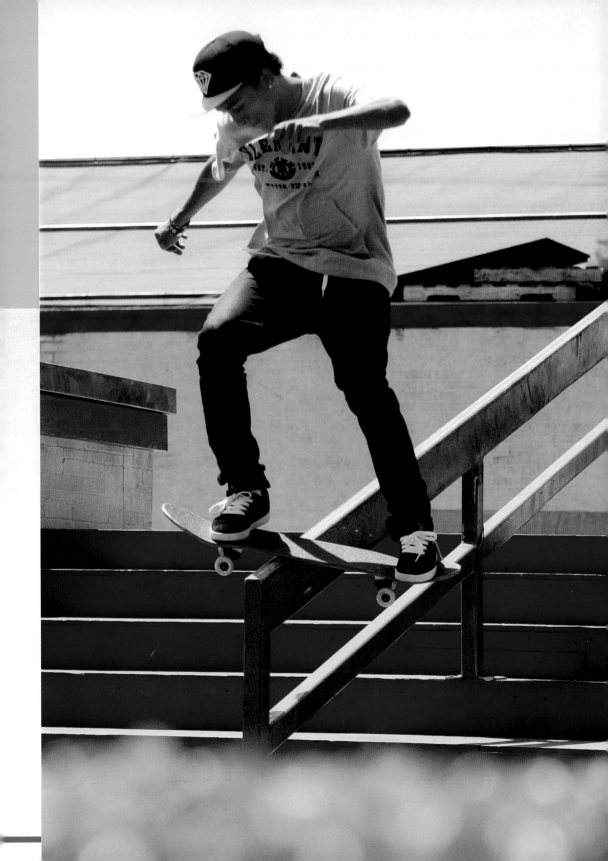

Huston was already a force on the Dew Action Sports Tour in 2006 at age 12. He notched his first X Games medal three years later. It only got better from there. Since 2010, Huston has dominated the Street League Skateboarding series, earning more prize money than any street skateboarder in history.

"The best part of being a professional skateboarder is making a living off of something that you have fun doing," Huston says. "I love my life. It's awesome."

Competitions are not all Huston does either. His skateboarding videos are among the most popular in the skateboarding community. Titles such as *Rise & Shine* and *Nyjah: Fade to Black* are among his many must-see videos for up-and-coming street skaters. Huston appears poised to be one of the biggest stars in skateboarding for years to come.

95.00

Nyjah Huston's final score for his second run of the street event at the 2014 Austin X Games—the highest street score in X Games history to date.

Nyjah Huston is one of the most influential young skateboarders in the world.

NYJAH HUSTON

Hometown: Davis, California

Height: 5 feet 10

Weight: 145 pounds

Birth Date: November 30, 1994

X Games: 5 gold medals
Street (2011)
Real Street (2012)
Street League (2013 Brazil, Spain, Los Angeles)

HONORABLE MENTIONS

Jamie Bestwick – The brightest star in BMX freestyle has won an amazing 12 X Games gold medals through 2014 and is famous for being the first to land big tricks, such as the double tailwhip flair.

Torah Bright – The Australian snowboarder rides slopestyle, superpipe, and even boardercross. She is a two-time gold medalist at the Winter X Games through 2014, and she also earned gold in the 2010 Winter Olympic halfpipe event.

Bob Burnquist – The skateboarding legend is known for his amazing creativity. Few action sports stars can match his longevity. Burnquist won his first X Games gold in 2000 and was still going strong when he won his twelfth gold medal in 2013.

Ricky Carmichael – As a supercross and motocross racer, Carmichael was all but unbeatable in the early 2000s. He won seven straight AMA Motocross titles. He also took home five AMA Supercross titles in that span.

Danny Harf – Harf may be the greatest wakeboarder of all time. The five-time national champion is famous for his biggest move, the double backflip.

Andy MacDonald – If not for Tony Hawk, MacDonald might be remembered as the greatest skateboarder of all time. MacDonald has an amazing 16 X Games medals—four of them gold.

Mike Metzger – The FMX pioneer helped launch the sport in the early 2000s. Fans loved his all-out style. He is most famous for his signature trick, the high-flying McMetz.

James Stewart – With five major AMA titles in supercross and motocross, Stewart was the first truly dominant black rider in US motor sports. From 2002 to 2014, he amassed 98 AMA wins.

GLOSSARY

barrel
The curved shape a wave makes as it crests.

boardercross
Also called snowboard cross, an event in which snowboarders race head-to-head down a mountain course.

freestyle
A type of sport in which contestants are scored based on tricks they perform.

slopestyle
A type of snowboarding competition in which riders perform tricks on an obstacle-filled downhill course.

snocross
A sport in which snowmobiles race over snow-covered bumps, jumps, and tight turns.

streetstyle
An event in skateboarding and BMX freestyle that takes place in a skatepark setting, with obstacles such as ramps and rails.

superpipe
An extra-large halfpipe used in snowboarding competitions.

vert
Short for *vertical*, vert is a skateboarding event that takes place in a vert ramp.

FOR MORE INFORMATION

Further Readings

Guillain, Charlotte. *Extreme Athletes: True Stories of Amazing Sporting Adventures*. Chicago: Raintree, 2014.

Hamilton, John. *Snowboarding*. Minneapolis, MN: Abdo Publishing, 2014.

Kissock, Heather (ed.). *Extreme Sports*. New York: AV2 by Weigl, 2013.

Websites

To learn more about Sports' Best Ever, visit **booklinks.abdopublishing.com**. These links are routinely monitored and updated to provide the most current information available.

INDEX

ABOUT THE AUTHOR

Matt Scheff is an author and artist living in Alaska. He enjoys mountain climbing, fishing, and curling up with his two Siberian huskies to watch sports.